MW00610059

Visit House Museums

CAPE COD, MARTHA'S VINEYARD & NANTUCKET

Marcia Young

Copyright © 2019 by Marcia Young

All rights reserved. This book or any portion thereof may not be reproduced or used in any manner whatsoever without the express written permission of the publisher except for the use of brief quotations in a book review.

Printed in the United States of America
First Printing, 2019

ISBN: 978-1-7339226-0-9 (print version)
        978-1-7339226-1-6 (ebook version)

Photographs are by the author, unless otherwise noted
Book cover and interior design by www.TeaBerryCreative.com
Index by Sarah Dubel
Map by Eureka Cartography

www.visithousemuseums.com

Acknowledgements

I want to thank my husband, Jack, for all the hours he spent going to house museums with me, reading house museum descriptions, sharing his technical talents and listening to me talk about this project for longer than I would like to admit. A special thanks to my daughter, Lauren, for creating my first website, answering my many, many technical questions and listening to me talk about house museums when history is not her thing. Thank you to my son, Justin, for not complaining too much when I dragged him to house museums when he was younger and supporting me throughout this project. Thank you to my sister, Dru, for reading almost every description in this book and giving me so many good suggestions. I would also like to thank Sharon Ingles, my best friend since first grade and an amazing editor who generously shared her 30 years of expertise with me.

Thank you to all the museum staff and volunteers who gave insightful tours, answered my endless questions and responded to my emails. In particular, I would like to thank the following people: from the Wing Fort House—Jim Grasela, Curator of the Wing Fort House and Memorial History Center, David Wheelock, Caretaker/Archaeologist; from the Benjamin Nye Homestead & Museum—John N. Cullity, Executive Director, Julia C. Hendy, Genealogist and Mary Kennan; from Falmouth Museums on the Green—Mark Schmidt, Executive Director; from the Swift-Daley House—Maureen Andujar, Curator and Vice-President of the Eastham Historical Society; from the Cobb House and the Harris-Black House—Sally Cabot Gunning, President of the Brewster Historical Society and amazing historical novelist; from the Crosby Mansion—Brian Locke, Property Manager; from the Centerville Historical Museum—Randall Hoel, Executive Director; from Highfield Hall—Janet Morgenstern Passani, Director of Marketing; from the Cahoon Museum of American Art—Sarah Johnson, PhD, Director; from the Phinney/Jones House—Betsy Wheeler, House Administrator; from the Penniman House—Sue Moynihan and Dani Crawford of the National Park Service, Cape Cod National Seashore; from the Osterville Historical Museum—Jennifer Morgan Williams, Executive Director; from the Taylor-Bray Farm—Bob Clark of the Taylor-Bray Farm Preservation Association; from the Captain Bangs Hallet House—Amy Heller, Administrator of the Historical Society of Old Yarmouth, Joel Chaison and Duncan Oliver, Co-Presidents of the Historical Society of Old Yarmouth and Barbara and Charlie Adams, House Collections Managers; from the Winslow Crocker House—Susanna Crampton, Public Relations Officer, Historic New England; from the Edward Gorey

House—Gregory Hischak, Curator and from the Atwood House & Museum—Danielle Jeanloz, Executive Director.

Thank you to Steven L. Markos of Art=Visual and Jeffrey Allen of Jeffrey Allen Photography on Nantucket for the use of their photographs and answering my questions about publishing, licenses and copyright. Thank you also to Jude Ahern of the Wellfleet Historical Society & Museum for his help with pictures of the Atwood-Higgins House. Thank you to Stace Curtis Wright from Eureka Cartography for the wonderful map. Thank you to Lindsey Teske for line editing. And thank you to "Brian from the Boat" for telling me about the Cahoon Museum of American Art and Barnstable Historical Society's Phinney/Jones House.

Lastly, to all my friends and extended family who have listened to me rattle on about house museums, "Thank you!"

Table of Contents

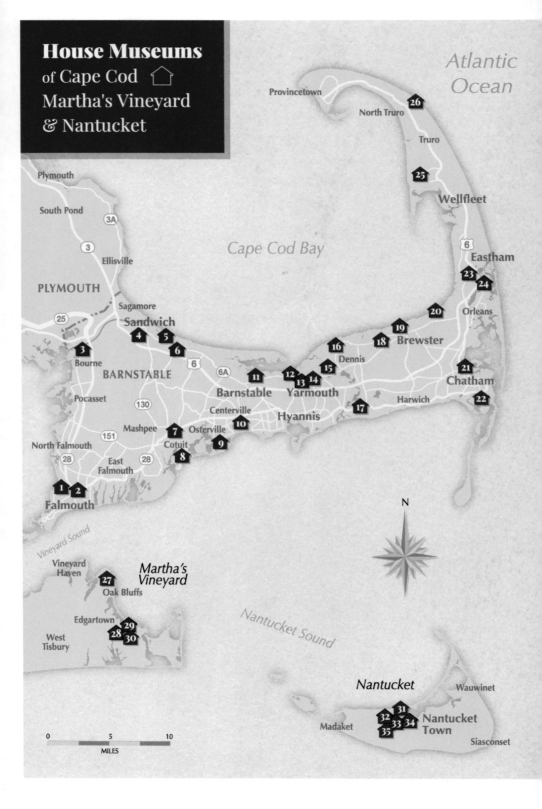

Map Locations

"*The sea-shore is a sort of neutral ground, a most advantageous point from which to contemplate this world.*"

—HENRY DAVID THOREAU, *Cape Cod*

Introduction

One of my fondest childhood memories is of a trip to Louisa May Alcott's house in Concord, Massachusetts. I spent an entire summer reading her book, *Little Women*. Going through the author's house brought the book to life in a way that was different from any I could have imagined. That was the beginning of my passion for house museums. Maybe you enjoy exploring the past the same way I do—wandering through the rooms other people lived in. I enjoy seeing children's toys, a writing desk or cooking utensils and imagining the everyday life of the people who used them.

Each house museum is a gem that has survived when others have not. Some survive because they are held in one family over a long period of time. Some survive due to the hard work of concerned citizens who are dedicated to historic preservation. Today, there are many house museums across the country that offer a glimpse into another life, another time. Look at the portraits in a historic house and you are looking at the Facebook of the past. Those people lived, loved and lost in these houses.

WHY CAPE COD?

Cape Cod is known for beautiful beaches and lazy summer days, but there is also a vast amount of history to explore. If you want to take a break from the beach or sneak in a bit of history along with your vacation, you do not have to go far.

The colonial history of New England literally starts at the tip of Cape Cod. Just about 400 years ago, the Pilgrims first stepped foot in the New World on the shores of what is known today as Provincetown. The Pilgrims eventually settled in Plymouth, but the Pilgrim Monument stands today in Provincetown to commemorate their first landing. Climbing the 252-foot tower is worth the effort for the spectacular view and to get an appreciation for what the English settlers saw as they sailed into what is now Provincetown Harbor.

This book includes descriptions of 35 house museums on Cape Cod, Martha's Vineyard and Nantucket. The houses range from those built in the 1600s to mansions built for entertaining members of high society. Each description includes a general overview of the museum along with practical information that will help when planning a visit.

Visitors can tour the homes of religious leaders, farmers, sea captains, artists and industrialists. Discover the rich maritime history of Cape Cod that includes the clipper ship era, the China Trade and the whaling industry. Many of the house museums on Cape Cod showcase the area's vibrant art community dating back to the early 1900s. Learn about the Native Americans who lived here thousands of years before the Pilgrims arrived. A tour of any one of these historic properties will transport you back in time and provide a glimpse into the life of those who lived there.

GENERAL INFORMATION

All museum contact and tour information is subject to change and should only be relied on as a general guide. Some house museums may close for private functions. For the most accurate information about any house museum, I strongly suggest that you call or visit the museum website before you go.

The information contained in this book has been gathered from my visits and the websites associated with each museum unless additional sources are noted. Whenever possible, my descriptions have been reviewed by representatives of the organization that maintains the museum. Hopefully, I have weeded out any glaring inaccuracies, but the purpose of this book is to provide an over-view of the museum, not to give a comprehensive history. I hope that your visit to any one of these historic properties will inspire you to learn more about the house and the people who lived there.

I do not include information on admission fees. Many museums ask for a donation rather than a fee. Fees often change. Check the museum website for current information on fees.

For purposes of this book, a house museum is a historic house that is open to the public a certain amount of time throughout the year. I also include one historic hotel in this book because it tells the story of the people who stayed there.

AVAILABILITY

Many house museums on Cape Cod are open only in the summer months when volunteers and tourists are plentiful. Some house museums stay open from Memorial Day to Columbus Day. A few house museums are open for most of the year.

The fall is considered "off-season" for Cape Cod, but it is my favorite time of year to visit. Always call or check the museum website before you plan your visit.

HELPFUL HINTS WHEN VISITING HOUSE MUSEUMS

- If the house is in a remote area, pack a lunch. Many house museums have surrounding grounds that are open to the public and perfect for a picnic.
- Wear sensible shoes. Many houses have uneven floors and steep stairs.
- Bring cash in small bills for admission fees or donations. Many houses will not have change on hand and do not take credit cards.
- When visiting an older house, consider bringing a small flashlight. The lighting in the house may not be very good, especially on cloudy days.

Photo opposite page: Barnstable Harbor

Cahoon Museum of American Art
c. 1782

4676 Falmouth Road (Route 28)
Cotuit, MA 02635
508-428-7581
https://cahoonmuseum.org

A visit to the Cahoon Museum of American Art combines both art and history. The museum is located in a historic home built in the late 1700s by the Crocker family. Five generations of Crockers lived in the house. Many of the original architectural features of the house have been preserved—the extensive paneling, the large cooking hearth, several fireplaces and the wide plank floors. In the early 1800s, the house became a tavern accommodating travelers arriving by stagecoach. The stenciling in the entry hallway is believed to be from this time period, as well as the hinged wall (complete with a door) on the second floor that could be raised to the ceiling or lowered to partition off the room.

In 1945, decorative furniture painters Ralph and Martha Cahoon bought this old colonial Georgian style house. They thought it would be the perfect place to showcase and sell their popular furniture and antiques. Several years later, one of their customers, Joan Whitney Payson, convinced the Cahoons to frame some of their art to exhibit in her gallery on Long Island. Their shows were a big success, and they soon made the transition from furniture to easel painting. Rather than working with canvas, they preferred creating their art on the hard, smooth surface of masonite which was more like the furniture they were accustomed to painting.

Ralph Cahoon's hallmark became his whimsical mermaids in nautical scenes with ships, lighthouses and whales as prominent features. Ralph's mermaids also have tea parties, go apple picking and playfully cavort in all sorts of fanciful situations. On display in the museum is Ralph's delightful *Bon Appétit* which he painted for the first on-air auction benefiting WGBH public television in Boston, featuring a mermaid resembling Julia Child adding wine to her pot as her mermaid assistants work nearby.

While Ralph used bold tones and vivid decoration to bring his scenes to life, Martha worked with a more muted palette. Martha featured mermaids in some of her work, but also painted still lifes and nature scenes evoking a simpler life gone by. Both artists were quite successful as American folk artists with sell-out exhibitions on Nantucket and in Palm Beach. Many of Cape Cod's famous visitors and summer residents purchased Cahoon paintings, including First Lady Jacqueline Kennedy.

After Ralph died in 1982, Rosemary Rapp, a Cotuit art collector, purchased the home with the intention of opening it as an art museum to showcase the Cahoons' work and her collection of early American art. The Cahoon Museum of American Art opened in 1984. It was a well-kept secret that Martha Cahoon continued to live in an apartment on the premises until her death in 1999.

The museum recently underwent an extensive renovation and expansion, reopening in May of 2016. The new exhibit space is bright and inviting, reflecting the essence of the attached antique homestead with the use of natural materials and adhering to the Cape Cod style of architecture. Rather than make the new addition blend in with the old house, the addition adds contrast with its natural cedar shingles trimmed in the same color as the house. This contrast is echoed in the museum itself as visitors move from the bright hickory floors found in the new addition to the dark wide plank floors of the original home, giving a subtle hint that they are stepping back in time.

The old Crocker House is the perfect backdrop for the Cahoons' decorative furniture and paintings. Their old studio is lovingly recreated in the room where they created their art. The museum's collection also consists of an impressive array of significant pieces of American art from early American to contemporary artists. The museum has several rotating special exhibits throughout the year. The gift shop highlights local artists and features gift items relating to the exhibits. Art lovers and history lovers are sure to enjoy their time spent at this wonderful museum.

AVAILABILITY:

- Open seasonally mid-March through mid-December: Tuesday through Saturday, 10am-4pm and Sunday, 1-4pm. Closed Mondays and major holidays.

NOTE: *Parking is behind the museum.*

Centerville Historical Museum
c. 1850 The Mary Lincoln House

---

513 Main Street
Centerville, MA 02632
508-775-0331
www.centervillehistoricalmuseum.org

J ust down Main Street from the iconic Four Seas Ice Cream and
1856 Country Store, visitors will find the Centerville Historical
Museum. It may not look like it from the outside, but inside the
museum visitors will find a historic house—the Mary Lincoln
House—built in the mid-1800s by Clark Lincoln. Mr. Lincoln had
a shop next door with general household and hardware items. His
first two wives died in their 30s. He had two daughters, one who
died at the age of 2 and the other, Mary Edward Lincoln, who lived

to be 87 years old. Mary lived in the house her father built until her death in 1955. She never married. The house remained largely unchanged during Mary's life, with no electricity and no plumbing until the last few years of her life.

The Centerville Historical Society acquired the house after Mary's death and opened it as a museum in 1955. The Society expanded the house in 1962 to accommodate its growing collections. A tour of the museum consists of three floors of exhibits and includes an extensive textile collection featuring gowns, uniforms, clothing and accessories from the 18th to the 20th century. There is also a maritime collection and a replica 1860s classroom. All of this is in addition to the historic home with its dining room, parlor and a colonial revival kitchen.

The museum is dedicated to preserving the history of Cape Cod and Centerville. There is so much to see in this 14-room museum—from toys and furniture to textiles and military items. With its extensive collections and several rotating exhibits, there is sure to be something of interest on display for every visitor.

AVAILABILITY:

- February through early December: Tuesday through Saturday, 12-4pm.

NOTE: *There are a few parking spots next to the building. Museum visitors can also park across the street at the Centerville Recreation Building.*

Dottridge Homestead
c. 1808

1148 Main Street
Cotuit, MA 02635
508-428-0461
www.cotuithistoricalsociety.org/homestead.html

The Dottridge Homestead was the home of Samuel and Abigail Dottridge and their seven children. Samuel worked as an apprentice learning carpentry in Brewster. When his apprenticeship was over, he married a local widow, Abigail. She owned this house which was built in the early 19th century. At the time, it was a three-room half Cape house. When Samuel and Abigail moved to Cotuit, the house was moved as well—by oxen. It took about three months, and they lived in the house as it moved. As their family grew, they added onto the house. The house has been moved several times, finally ending up in its current location.

The house has been restored to reflect how it might have looked when Samuel and Abigail lived there. Each room is furnished with period furniture, clothing and household items. There is an extensive family tree over the fireplace showing the descendants of Samuel and Abigail. There is an exposed section of an original wall illustrating construction methods of the early 1800s and a kitchen garden reminiscent of the period. On the property, there is also an ice house built in the late 1800s with an attached privy that was added later.

Behind the homestead, is the Cotuit Museum which has exhibits highlighting the history of Cotuit and its people. One popular exhibit is the recreated doctor's office of Dr. Donald Higgins who practiced family medicine in Cotuit. Visitors can also see antique firefighting equipment and the oldest mechanized fire engine on Cape Cod in the William Morse Fire Museum.

AVAILABILITY:

- Memorial Day to Christmas: Friday, Saturday and Sunday, 1-5pm.
- Check the website for additional events.

Osterville Historical Museum

c. 1728 Cammett House

c. 1824 Captain Parker House

c. 1855 Herbert F. Crosby Boat Shop

155 West Bay Road

Osterville, MA 02655

508-428-5861

https://ostervillemuseum.org

Less than half a mile from the center of Osterville, visitors can explore the two-acre campus of the Osterville Historical Museum. It is an unexpected treat to discover how many treasures are tucked away at this museum—two historic houses, an 1850s boat shop, more than a dozen full-sized wooden boats and recently discovered murals painted nearly a century ago by a local artist.

The Cammett House is believed to be the oldest house in Osterville. It was built in the early 1700s as a modest one-room deep house. The kitchen and an extension on the house were added in the 1800s. The original underpinnings of the house can be seen from a viewing area open to the basement. The house is named after John Cammett, a fisherman, and his family who lived in this house in the early to mid-1800s. The house has been brought back to the days of the Cammett family including an herb garden just outside the kitchen door.

The Parker House was built in 1824 by Captain Jonathan Parker, a schooner captain. The house has been added onto since then and is now the home of the Osterville Historical Museum. The Museum's collections relating to Osterville include artwork, ceramics and furniture along with rotating exhibits. A recent addition to the Museum's collection is the newly discovered landscape murals of Vernon Coleman. Found during a renovation of a local restaurant, the murals depict the seaside beauty of the Cape from the 1920s on. Coleman was an art teacher on Cape Cod for over 25 years.

Boating enthusiasts will delight in learning the history of the Crosby family boat building tradition—an Osterville family that has been building and maintaining their iconic wooden boats for over two centuries. Visitors can tour the 1855 Herbert F. Crosby Boat Shop and the adjoining boat sheds which are home to the largest collection of full-sized wooden boats in Massachusetts, including the Wianno Senior, the Wianno Junior, skiffs and catboats. Even those who do not sail are sure to remember seeing photographs of President John F. Kennedy and his family sailing his Wianno Senior in the waters off Hyannis Port. Many visitors may also remember learning to sail in a Beetle Cat—known for being particularly difficult to capsize.

Children can play in the Jelly House located on the grounds. Tourists would stop along the road to buy beach plum jelly at one of these tiny "houses." When they fell out of favor, they were sold to individuals to use as play houses. This one is the perfect size for little visitors to enjoy.

AVAILABILITY:

- Mid-June to mid-October: Thursday through Saturday, 10am-2pm.
- Check the website for special events throughout the year.

NOTES: *Parking is in back of the museum off Parker Road. Farmers Market is on Fridays from 9am to 1pm in season.*

Phinney/Jones House

Barnstable Historical Society Museum

c. 1834

3087 Main Street (Route 6A)

Barnstable, MA 02630

508-362-2982

www.barnstablehistoricalsociety.org

Just west of the bustling center of quaint Barnstable Village, visitors will find the Phinney/Jones House. The house was built by Sylvanus B. Phinney in the early 1800s. Phinney was the founder and editor of *The Barnstable Patriot*, a weekly local newspaper that continues today. The house was purchased by the Barnstable Historical Society in 2012 and now serves as the Society's museum.

The Society is dedicated to preserving the history of all seven villages of Barnstable.

Visitors to the Phinney/Jones House can tour two floors of rooms, each telling a story. There is the dining room and parlor downstairs and bedrooms upstairs. Visitors learn about the maritime history of the Cape and the many clipper ship captains who called Barnstable home. The home is filled with artifacts from the China Trade, portraits, clipper ship paintings and personal items. In the dining room, visitors can imagine how a captain's wife might have entertained with the vast array of porcelain china and silver on display. The children's room upstairs is filled with antique dolls, toys, clothes and furniture providing a glimpse into daily family life in the 1800s. There is an antique tool display and even a butterfly collection. Each visitor is sure to find something that piques their interest in the history of Barnstable and Cape Cod.

AVAILABILITY:

- Mid-June to mid-October: Wednesday through Saturday from 1-4pm.
- Check the website for the date of the annual Holiday House Tour and other events.

Briggs–McDermott House
c. 1830

22 Sandwich Road
Bourne, MA 02532
508-759-6120
www.bournepreservation.org

The Briggs-McDermott House is located across from the public library. This Greek Revival style house has been restored to reflect life in the mid-1800s to the early 1900s. Each room of the house has been historically reproduced allowing visitors to experience life in Bourne in earlier times. Of particular note is the music room ceiling which was painted in the late 1800s by famed marine artist and Bourne resident Charles Raleigh. The ceiling has been recently restored bringing it back to its original glory.

The house is furnished with period pieces, personal items and a vintage clothing collection.

Also open to the public are the Alonzo Booth Blacksmith Shop and the Allen Green Carriage House. Visitors can see a working forge in the blacksmith shop and vintage carriages and sleighs on display in the carriage house.

AVAILABILITY:

- Mid-June through August: Guided tours Friday and Saturday, 1-4pm.
- Check the website for special events throughout the year. The annual holiday open house is held in December.
- Appointments for tours at other times can be made by calling 508-759-6120.

Cobb House
1799

739 Lower Road

Brewster, MA 02631

508-896-9521

www.brewsterhistoricalsociety.org

The Cobb House is a grand ship captain's home built by Elijah Cobb in 1799. The Brewster Historical Society acquired the house in 2015, restoring and renovating it while keeping as much of the original architectural features as possible. Visitors can see the original beehive oven used for baking along with the original Rumford fireplaces throughout the house. The formal parlor—used mostly for visitors—has extensive dentil molding and interior shutters on the windows that disappear into the walls when not in use.

The front staircase was quite grand for the day and the front door and lock are original, although the stenciling is from a later period.

A tour of the Cobb House consists of two floors. The first floor includes the keeping room and two parlors. On display are items from the clipper ship era, including a sea captain's medicine chest and a first mate's desk, and family treasures from the China Trade. The front staircase serves as a gallery for portraits and ship paintings.

On the second-floor landing, visitors can see one of the prize possessions of the Society, the first known photograph of Helen Keller and Anne Sullivan. It is the only known photograph of Keller with her doll which is significant because "doll" was the first word that the blind and deaf Keller learned as Sullivan spelled it out into her hand. The photo was taken by Cornelius Chenery in 1888 when he was a boarder at the Cobb House and Keller and Sullivan were summering in Brewster.

The second floor includes the master bedroom and a second less formal bedroom. In the master bedroom, visitors will see items from the museum's textile collection, personal items and children's toys and furniture. The second bedroom is called the Brewster Room and includes items from the Society's collection that bring to life the history of the town of Brewster, including an original ballot box and the old East Brewster Post Office. The rest of the house serves as the offices of the Society.

Visitors can also enjoy the beautiful garden in the back of the Cobb House. The Society recreated the garden using descriptions found in the diary of Captain Cobb's great-granddaughter, Caroline

Atherton Dugan, as a guide. The Society used heirloom seeds wherever possible.

AVAILABILITY:

- Late June to beginning of September: Wednesday, 4-7pm and Thursday through Saturday, 1-4pm. Memorial Day through Columbus Day: Saturdays, 1-4pm.
- Check the website for specific dates and special events.

NOTES: *Parking area is behind the house. Free audio tour app is available.*

Crosby Mansion
1888

163 Crosby Lane
Brewster, MA 02631
508-896-1744
www.crosbymansion.com

Just a short ride from Route 6A, visitors may be surprised to come upon a yellow and white mansion with a grand front porch lined with Romanesque arches. This three-story mansion was built by Albert Crosby for his second wife, Matilda. It was completed in 1888. A century later, this once beautiful mansion was vacant and beset by vandals. In 1992, a dedicated group of volunteers convinced the Commonwealth of Massachusetts to let them renovate and restore the property rather than having it torn down.

The Friends of Crosby Mansion have worked tirelessly to bring the mansion back to life.

Albert Crosby was born and raised in Brewster in a modest home which still stands on the same property as the mansion today. In fact, the mansion was built around Crosby's old homestead. It is said that he would retreat to his old, familiar home for some peace and quiet when his wife's parties became too much for him.

Mr. Crosby left the Cape as a young man, settling in Chicago. He made his fortune producing distilled alcohol and selling the medicinal alcohol to the army during the Civil War. Suffice it to say, that Albert had quite a colorful life—making and losing lots of money, divorcing his first wife, Margaret, who returned to Massachusetts with their four children and marrying Matilda, a former burlesque singer twenty years his junior. Matilda and Albert traveled through Europe for ten years and then returned to Chicago for a few more years before finally returning to Brewster after the death of both of Albert's parents.

Upon his return to the Cape, Albert spared no expense building a lavish 35-room home for his wife who was used to the bright lights and excitement of show business and the finer things in life. It had 15 fireplaces, gas heating and lighting, hand carved mahogany and oak walls, marble in the baths, a billiard room and a two-story art gallery with skylights to keep the sun from shining directly on their extensive art collection. The extravagant mansion was the perfect backdrop for entertaining the luminaries of the day, including Samuel Clemens (perhaps better known by his pen name, Mark Twain), John Barrymore, the Duke of Wales and Helen Keller.

Albert died at home in 1906. Matilda continued to spend summers at the mansion with her sister and niece. Upon Matilda's death in 1928, the property was divided between her two grandnieces. They took what personal items they wanted from the house and sold the rest, including a Bierstadt painting which they sold for $250 on the front lawn that today is worth millions. The painting now hangs in the Birmingham Museum of Art. Subsequently, the mansion was used as a music school, a restaurant and a diet camp for young women. Eventually, the mansion was abandoned.

Today, the work of restoring the mansion continues. The Friends of Crosby Mansion open the mansion for open houses four times each summer as well as special events. A tour consists of two floors, with spectacular views of the bay from the second floor. Visitors appreciate the workmanship that went into the building of this mansion as they tour the parlor, the billiards room, the dining room and the library. Visitors also see the original homestead that was retained when the mansion was built. Unfortunately, the two-story art gallery burned in 1952. Even so, a tour of the mansion lets visitors imagine what life was like in high society on Cape Cod in the late 1800s and the early 1900s.

AVAILABILITY:

- Four open houses in the summer from 10am-2pm.
- Check the website for open house dates and special events.

ADDITIONAL SOURCE:

"The Crosby Mansion: From Yesteryear to Present", Booklet created by "Friends" Volunteers: Historian and Author, Cathi Pivnicny and Editor, Cathy Jewett.

Harris–Black House

c. 1795

Windmill Village in Drummer Boy Park

773 Main Street (Route 6A)

Brewster, MA 02631

508-896-9521

www.brewsterhistoricalsociety.org/brewster-historical-society-visit

The Harris-Black House is located within Drummer Boy Park. Built in the late 18th century, this modest one-room house was once home to a blacksmith and his large family. A tour of the Harris-Black House offers a glimpse into the life and living conditions of an everyday family living on Cape Cod at the time. Visitors can also tour the Higgins Farm Windmill and see black-smith demonstrations in the Hopkins Blacksmith Shop. Adjacent walking trails and children's playground make this a good stop for all ages.

AVAILABILITY:

- Late June through Labor Day: Fridays and Saturdays, 12-3pm. Memorial Day through Columbus Day: Saturdays, 12-3pm.
- Check the website for specific dates and special events.

NOTE: *Free audio tour app is available.*

Atwood House & Museum
c. 1750s

347 Stage Harbor Road
Chatham, MA 02633
508-945-2493
https://chathamhistoricalsociety.org

The Atwood House has been preserved in almost its original form and is now part of the Atwood House & Museum. The house was built in the mid-1750s by Captain Joseph Atwood as a full Cape with two windows on either side of the center door. It has a gambrel roof which means that there is more room on the second floor than in a house with the typical slanted roof. This was a grand house at the time it was built—fit for a ship captain and substantial land owner.

In 1833, a new wing was added to the house for Margery Atwood, second wife of John Atwood, Joseph Atwood's grandson. As the story goes, Margery was promised a new house before she married John and was not happy with the idea of adding onto the old house. The addition added the summer kitchen. Margery also received her own entrance and her own bedroom. She lived in the house until her death in 1888. John died in 1864. Visitors are left to wonder a bit about the state of their marriage, but no one can truly know.

The original two-story house has four rooms on the first floor—parlor, sitting room, sink room and kitchen. The second floor has a large bedroom with a fireplace, but it is no longer open to the public. The two front rooms are restored as they might have been in the mid-1800s. The kitchen includes a beehive oven used for baking—the typical "beehive" shape of the back of the oven can be seen from the adjacent closet. There is also a borning room next to the fireplace—a warm, cozy place for mother and newborn to keep warm.

Also on the grounds of the museum is the Nickerson North Beach Camp which was saved from erosion on the barrier beach in Chatham. Floated on a barge and then put on a flatbed truck, the camp was moved to this location in 1991 together with its outhouse. Built in the 1940s, it was used by the Joshua Nickerson family as a summer "cottage." With no electricity or heat, the camp harkens back to the simple pleasures of camping out on the barrier beaches. The camp was donated to the museum intact, complete with furniture, dishes, tools and even liquor bottles over the ice box.

The Atwood House & Museum serves as the headquarters of the Chatham Historical Society and houses extensive exhibits preserving the history of Cape Cod and the town of Chatham. There are several rotating and permanent exhibits—from maritime history and the commercial fishing industry to local tools and textiles to seashells, carved birds and Sandwich Glass. There is something of interest for every visitor.

One compelling exhibit tells the true story of the rescue of the SS *Pendleton* which was depicted in the movie, *The Finest Hours*. On February 18, 1952, the SS *Pendleton*, an oil tanker, broke in two off the coast of Chatham. Four Coast Guardsmen from the Chatham Lifeboat Station risked their lives and saved 31 of the crew in a boat designed to carry only 12 people. It is called the greatest rescue by a small boat in Coast Guard history.

Another unique exhibit is found in the Mural Barn displaying the murals of local artist, Alice Stallknecht Wight. The murals depict actual Chatham residents from the 1930s and 1940s. Stallknecht's paintings are hard to describe, to say the least. Striking and bold, they show ordinary people in ordinary situations. Some might say Stallknecht's technique is reminiscent of Van Gogh, while others see a German expressionist influence. In any case, this stunning exhibit is a surprising departure from the usual collections of historical societies. While the old Atwood House is a focal point of the museum and a destination in and of itself, once at the museum, visitors will find that there is so much else to see.

AVAILABILITY:

- Memorial Day Weekend: Friday and Saturday, 1-5pm. Late May through June: Tuesday through Saturday, 1-5pm. July and August: Tuesday through Saturday, 10am-5pm. September through October: Tuesday through Saturday, 1-5pm.
- Check the website for specific dates and special events throughout the year.
- Group tours can be arranged year-round by calling the museum.

Caleb Nickerson Homestead

c. 1829

1107 Orleans Road (Route 28)

Chatham, MA 02633

508-945-6086

https://nickersonassoc.com

Caleb Nickerson's home, built in the early 19th century, sits on the two-acre campus of the Nickerson Family Association. The house was saved from demolition and moved to its current location in 2003. The house has been restored to reflect life in the early 1800s with period furnishings. Many of the original architectural features of the home have been preserved. The home has three hearths and a working beehive oven. There is also a reproduction post-and-beam outhouse on the property.

The Nickerson Family Association is dedicated to the research of the descendants of William Nickerson (1604-1689), the founder of Chatham. The Association's Genealogical Research Center currently contains information on more than 350,000 descendants of William Nickerson. A Nickerson Family Association reunion is held every year.

The Research Center is located on land originally owned by William Nickerson. A very active archeological dig is ongoing, and researchers believe they have found the original site of the home built by William Nickerson circa 1664. The corners of the house and the remnants of the hearth have been unearthed along with artifacts that will be studied by archeologists to help us better understand the life of the early settlers of Cape Cod.

AVAILABILITY:

- June through September: Wednesday and Saturday, 10-2:00pm.
- Check the website for specific opening and closing dates and special events, including the Annual Holiday Hearthside Open House.

Jericho Historical Center

Sea Captain Theophilus Baker's 1801 Home

c. 1801

90 Old Main Street

West Dennis, MA 02670

508-385-2232 • 508-398-8592

www.dennishistsoc.org/Museums/Museums-01-Jericho.html

This full Cape style house with two windows on either side of the front door and a steep roof was built in 1801 by sea captain Theophilus Baker. It was occupied by members of the Baker family until 1955. For over a century and a half, no significant renovations or improvements were done to the house—not even the installation of heat or electricity. When Elizabeth Reynard, herself a Baker descendent, bought the old dilapidated house, she intended to renovate the house and live in it.[1] Unfortunately, after completing many of the renovations, her health declined and she never realized her dream of living there. After her death, according to her wishes, the house was donated to the town of Dennis to use as a historical center.

Today, the house contains period furnishings, textiles, paintings, toys and personal items that bring visitors back to the simpler days of the 1800s. In the Barn Museum behind the house, visitors are treated to an array of antique tools from industries found on Cape Cod in the 19th century—cranberry harvesting, saltworks, carpentry and farming. A reproduction general store reminds visitors of the importance of the neighborhood store—not just as a place to purchase everyday necessities, but also as a community gathering place.

AVAILABILITY:

- Late June to early September: Tuesday and Thursday from 1-4pm.
- Check the website for specific dates and special events, including the Annual Pie Baking Contest and the Christmas Afternoon Tea.

---

1   Nicole Muller. "'Tea and Talk' at Jericho in West Dennis". *The Register*. Posted Feb. 6, 2014. Updated Feb. 7, 2014. http://capecod.wickedlocal.com/article/20140206/News/140208243

Josiah Dennis Manse

c. 1736

61 Whig Street
Dennis, MA 02638
508-385-2232
www.dennishistsoc.org/Museums/Museums-02-Josiah.html

Situated in a lovely residential area north of Route 6A, this salt-box house was home to Josiah Dennis. He was the first minister of the parish of the East Precinct of Yarmouth (which later became the town of Dennis) and the man for whom the town was named. The original part of the house was built in the 1690s. An addition was added around 1736.

After the last member of the Dennis family passed away, members of the Howes family lived in the house for over 200 years.

Many of the historic items displayed in the house have been donated to the museum by the Howes family, including furniture, clothing, toys and paintings. With displays of period furnishings and personal items, the house offers a glimpse into life in the mid-1700s. Visitors can explore two parlors and the keeping room on the first floor. There is also a children's room, a maritime wing and spinning and weaving exhibits. In addition to the house, there is a one room schoolhouse on the grounds dating to around 1745.

AVAILABILITY:

- Late June through August: Tuesday, 10am-1pm; Thursday, 1-4pm; some Saturdays 1-4pm.
- Check the website for specific dates and special events, including Colonial Day at the Manse, Autumn at the Manse and Christmas at the Manse.

NOTES:
- *Entrance to the Manse is on Nobscusset Road.*
- *Nearby and worth a visit is Scargo Tower (152 Scargo Hill Road, Dennis)—a 30-foot high stone observation tower built in 1901. Climb the steep spiral staircase and experience spectacular views of Scargo Lake and Cape Cod Bay. On a clear day, visitors can see from Plymouth to Provincetown. It's a little tricky to find, but worth the effort.*

Penniman House
1868

170 Fort Hill Road
(Intersection of Fort Hill and Governor Prence Roads)
Eastham, MA 02642
508-255-3421
www.nps.gov/caco/learn/historyculture/penniman.htm

The Penniman House was built by Captain Edward Penniman in 1868 and occupied by members of the Penniman family until the death of Captain Penniman's daughter, Betsy, in 1957. Betsy's niece, Irma Penniman Broun inherited the house and sold it to the National Park Service in 1963.

This two-and-a-half story house is a wonderful example of fine craftsmanship and high-end finishes fitting for a successful whaling captain and his family. The house offers a glimpse into the technology available in the mid to late 1800s. The house was built with indoor plumbing, and a coal-fired furnace was installed in the 1890s. The house is not fully furnished, but a few rooms are restored with Penniman family items to reflect the life and times when the captain and his family occupied the house. Pictures taken in the early 1900s provide a window into the life of the Penniman family.

AVAILABILITY:

- July to September: Call Salt Pond Visitor Center (508-255-3421) to confirm dates and times.

NOTES:

- *A small parking lot is beyond the house on Fort Hill Road.*
- *While the Penniman House is known for its whalebone gate welcoming visitors, the gate has been removed due to its deterioration. The Park Service is reviewing options for a possible replacement.*
- *Access the Fort Hill Trail from the parking lot—about a 1-mile loop trail with marsh views. Dogs are not allowed.*

Swift–Daley House
1741

2375 State Highway (Route 6)

Eastham, MA 02642

(Next to the Post Office)

508-240-8071

https://www.easthamhistoricalsociety.org/swift-daley-museum

The Swift-Daley House was built by Joshua Knowles in 1741. This house, with its bowed roof, is typical of houses built by ships' carpenters living on Cape Cod at the time. Many of the original architectural features of the house have survived, such as the wide board floors, original wainscoting, deep kitchen fireplace and narrow, steep stairs. The rooms have been furnished using period pieces to bring to life the many generations that lived in the house from the Colonial period to the Victorian era.

On the same site as the Swift-Daley House is the A. Thomas Dill Beach Camp, built in 1936. It is one of several small camps which dotted Eastham's Coast Guard Beach. Dill Beach Camp was the only camp to survive the brutal Blizzard of '78. It was moved to its present location in 1995. It is furnished exactly as it would have been when it was used as a fishing and hunting camp. With no electricity and no modern plumbing, it harkens back to a simpler time.

The Ranlett Tool Museum, located behind the Swift-Daley House, is a treasure trove of antique tools. On display are hundreds of unique tools relating to local industries such as fishing, cranberry harvesting, carpentry and so much more. A working forge is fired up once or twice a year.

AVAILABILITY:

- July and August: Wednesday through Friday, 10am-1pm.
- Check the website for specific dates and special events. Also open Saturday of Windmill Weekend in September.

NOTE: *The entrance is easy to miss. The house is located next to the post office.*

Falmouth Museums on the Green

c. 1730 Conant House
1790 Dr. Francis Wicks House

65 Palmer Avenue
Falmouth, MA 02540
508-548-4857
http://museumsonthegreen.org

The two-acre campus of the Falmouth Museums on the Green includes two historic houses—the Wicks House and the Conant House—along with the Hallett Barn Visitors Center and the Cultural Center. Visitors start at the Visitors Center which features rotating exhibits and displays relating to Falmouth and its people. From there, visitors can take a guided tour of the Wicks House.

The center-entrance Federal style house was built in 1790 by Dr. Francis Wicks. It was the most elegant house on the village green at the time. Dr. Wicks, along with another Falmouth doctor, Dr. Hugh Donaldson, was instrumental in persuading the town of Falmouth to approve inoculation against smallpox in 1797. Each of the rooms of the house have been reproduced with furnishings representing the Colonial through Victorian eras. Walking through this house offers a glimpse into how a successful doctor and his family lived in the late 1700s and early 1800s. Displays of antique medical tools allow visitors to imagine what the practice of medicine entailed during that time. It is understandable if visitors also come away with a new appreciation for modern medicine.

Visitors can tour the Conant House on their own. The exact date when the house was built is not known, but it is believed to be the oldest house still in existence on the village green. The historic district where the house sits dates back to about 1730. Some of the interior structure may indicate that it was built as late at the last quarter of the 1700s. In any case, this historic property was purchased by the Falmouth Historical Society in 1966 and restored to a typical 1700s half Cape dwelling. Part of the house serves as archives and offices of the Historical Society. Visitors are welcome to wander through the rest of the house which includes exhibits reflecting life in Falmouth through the years. One of the most engaging exhibits is a video made from silent movie footage shot in 1941 offering a unique window into a simpler time in the life of the residents of Falmouth.

A trip to the Falmouth Museums on the Green is not complete without spending some time exploring the extensive gardens on the property lovingly maintained by the Falmouth Garden Club— the Colonial Garden, the Colonial Herb Garden and the Memorial Park which is dotted with small signs each containing a fascinating tidbit relating to Falmouth. There is even a small replica of the old schoolhouse attended by famous Falmouth resident, Katherine Lee Bates, author of *America the Beautiful*. The schoolhouse is big enough for children to play in and painted on the inside with chalkboard paint so they can even write on the walls.

AVAILABILITY:

- Early June to early October: Monday through Friday, 10am-3pm; Saturday 10am-1pm.
- Check the website for specific dates and special events.

NOTE: *There are a few parking spots in front of the Visitors Center and a parking lot behind the Cultural Center which can be entered from Katherine Lee Bates Road.*

Highfield Hall
1878

56 Highfield Drive
Falmouth, MA 02540
508-495-1878
https://highfieldhallandgardens.org

Highfield Hall is hidden in the woods just a short drive from Main Street in Falmouth. This summer "cottage" was built in 1878 by a wealthy Bostonian, Pierson Beebe. The nearly 18,000 square foot mansion was one of the first summer estates to be built on Cape Cod. It was built in the ornate Queen Anne Stick style popular in the late 1800s with extensive detailed exterior wood trim and steep roofs. The mansion has 157 windows in 31 unique styles and 10 stained glass windows.

Unfortunately, the property fell into decline after the last of the Beebe family died. When the house was about to be demolished, a group of local citizens formed a non-profit organization, Historic Highfield, Inc., intent on saving the house. With the help of the town of Falmouth, the house was saved and restored to its former glory.

The architectural details of the house have been beautifully restored. High-end workmanship is evident in the detailed mantels, staircases and moldings. The house has one room dedicated to the history of the house and the Beebe family. The rest of the house is a canvas for rotating art exhibits showcasing the work of local, national and international artists.

The gardens have been restored with dedication and attention to the past. The beautiful grounds of the property are a lovely setting for a picnic. You can access the trails of the Beebe Woods from the rear of the property. Beebe Woods was once part of this 700-acre property, but now is owned by the town of Falmouth. Whether a visitor is interested in the ornate architecture of the mansion or is an art lover who appreciates viewing an art exhibit in a unique setting or a nature lover who wants to experience the gardens and hike in the adjacent woods, Highfield Hall offers all of that and more.

AVAILABILITY:

- April 15 to October 31: Tuesday through Friday, 10am-4pm; Saturday and Sunday, 10am-2pm. Monday closed except for holidays. Open Memorial Day, Labor Day and Columbus Day. July and August: Free Fridays 4-7pm.

- Docent-led estate tours free with admission: First and third Sunday of the month from May through mid-October, 12:30-1:30pm, weather permitting.
- Check the website for specific dates and special events such as Holidays at Highfield in late November and early December.

NOTES: *The grounds are open daily year-round from dawn to dusk. The museum may be closed for private functions.*

Cooke House
c. 1732

59 School Street
Edgartown, MA 02539
508-627-4441
http://www.mvmuseum.org/visit.php#hours

The Cooke House is believed to be the oldest structure on Martha's Vineyard still standing on its original site. The house was built by Temple Phillips Cooke around 1732. While not a lot is known about him, he is believed to have had legal training. One of his sons became a judge and held court in this house. A grandson became a customs officer and is believed to have had his customs office in one of the upstairs rooms.

Visitors can tour the 1815 summer kitchen, the keeping room with its original fireplace, the room used by the judge to hold court and the parlor with museum collection items displayed to represent life in the mid 1800s. The Cooke family moved out of the house in 1851, taking their possessions with them. However, several early period household items were excavated from underneath the house and are on display.

AVAILABILITY:

- The Martha's Vineyard Museum will close on Labor Day in 2018 to relocate to its new permanent location at the historic Vineyard Haven Marine Hospital.
- The Cooke House is scheduled to reopen in summer 2019. Call the museum or check the website for hours.

Cottage Museum
late 1800s

1 Trinity Park
Oak Bluffs
Martha's Vineyard, MA 02557
508-693-0525
508-693-5042
http://www.mvcma.org/cottage-museum--shop.html

Just a five-minute walk from the docks of Oak Bluffs Harbor, visitors will find the most unique neighborhood on Martha's Vineyard—the iconic gingerbread houses of the Martha's Vineyard Camp Meeting Association. While the cottages are privately owned, one is open to the public—the Cottage Museum which is dedicated to preserving the history of the neighborhood and the religious movement from which it came.

The religious camp meeting movement was started in the early 1800s by Presbyterians on the American frontier. People would come from great distances, typically for a week, to hear a preacher and practice their religion with others. Conditions were primitive and members would stay in tents. The movement spread to New England with the Methodists holding their own meetings. The first camp meeting held on Martha's Vineyard was in 1835. Three decades later, there were over 500 tents at what was then called "Wesleyan Grove." Rather than staying for just a week, people began staying longer to enjoy the island's sea air and beautiful surroundings. Wanting more permanent accommodations, small wooden buildings began to replace the tents. Today there are over 300 of those tiny wooden cottages remaining in this charming 34-acre community.

The cottages were built in a style reminiscent of the tents they replaced. The smaller side of the cottage faces the street. The double front doors resemble tent flaps and are mirrored above by the double doors leading to the upstairs balcony. The cottages were built in a unique gingerbread style with distinctive filigree woodwork attributed to local carpenters. The first floor was for socializing and up the steep, narrow stairway, the second floor was for sleeping. Stepping inside the Cottage Museum visitors can imagine what life might have been like in this tiny cottage in the late 1800s to early 1900s. An assortment of personal items and historical artifacts are on display in the first and second floors of the cottage. There is also a small gift shop.

Visitors are welcome to explore the neighborhood but should not enter any yards or cottages. They are all privately owned. Unless there is an event going on inside, visitors are also encouraged to explore the Tabernacle which is at the heart of the neighborhood. The Tabernacle was originally planned as a wooden structure, but the cost was prohibitive. The decision was made to construct a wrought iron structure which was much more cost effective. The Tabernacle was built within a matter of months. The contract for its construction was finalized in April 1879, and the first service was held only a few months later, on July 26, 1879. Today, the Tabernacle stands as one of the finest examples of a wrought iron structure in the United States.

AVAILABILITY:

- Memorial Day through mid-October: Monday through Saturday, 10am-4pm; Sunday, 1-4pm.
- Check the website for dates and times of special events such as the Annual Gingerbread Cottage Tour—an opportunity to see inside several privately-owned gingerbread cottages.
- Walking tours—July and August: Tuesday and Thursday, 11am. Walking tours start at the Tabernacle.

NOTES:

- *The Tabernacle is a place of worship. No food or beverages are allowed inside.*
- *The cottages are privately owned. Do not enter any yards, porches or cottages.*

Dr. Daniel Fisher House
1840

99 Main Street

Edgartown, MA 02539

508-627-4440

http://mvpreservation.org/properties/dr-daniel-fisher-house/

This elegant Federal style home was built in 1840 by Dr. Daniel Fisher, a doctor and a businessman. During the height of the whaling industry, Dr. Fisher was one of the richest men in the country. At the turn of the 20th century, Senator William Morgan Butler acquired the home. During Senator Butler's ownership, several significant architectural and landscaping features were added to the house, including the beautiful semi-circular porch on the east side and the car port on the west side.

After being used for office space for many years, the house was renovated in 1992 and restored to its earlier glory. The house is currently used as event space for weddings and private functions. When not in use, the house is included in the Architectural Walking Tour of the Vineyard Trust. A tour of the Fisher House introduces visitors to the elegance of this historic house with its intricate moldings, grand staircase and generous rooms. The beautiful gardens, including a sunken water garden, have been lovingly restored and are worth a visit.

AVAILABILITY:

- Late spring through October: Wednesday through Sunday, a tour of the Fisher House is included in the Architectural Walking Tour of the Vineyard Trust which begins at 10:30am and 2pm. Purchase tickets at The Carnegie located at 58 North Water St., Edgartown. The walking tour lasts about 90 minutes, beginning at The Carnegie and ending at the Vincent House less than a half mile away. Call to confirm tour times.

NOTES:

- *If there is a private function at the Fisher House, the interior of the house will not be included in the walking tour.*

- *A bit of information on The Carnegie (58 North Water St., Edgartown)—The Carnegie is where visitors purchase tickets for the walking tour and where the tour starts. The building previously housed the town library which was originally funded by Andrew Carnegie. It was recently renovated and opened as the museum of the Vineyard Trust—dedicated to preserving the history of Martha's Vineyard and its people. Visitors should plan to spend some time exploring the excellent exhibits of The Carnegie before or after the walking tour.*

- *Visitors might want to wander down Daggett Street directly across from The Carnegie to watch the Chappy Ferry travel the 527 feet from Edgartown Memorial Wharf to Chappaquiddick Island and back again.*

Vincent House Museum
c. 1672

99A Main Street
Edgartown, MA 02539
508-627-4440
http://mvpreservation.org/properties/vincent-house-museum/

The Vincent House is believed to be the island's oldest exist-
ing residence. Built in the late 1600s, this home was originally
located on 20 acres of farmland along the shores of Edgartown
Great Pond. It was continuously owned by members of the Vincent
family until 1940. The house was moved to its current location
after it was donated to the Martha's Vineyard Preservation Trust
(now known as the Vineyard Trust).

71

The house retains its original footprint and many architecturally significant original features. The house is furnished with period antiques and reproduction pieces reflecting life on the island from the 1600s to the 1900s. Some of the furnishings in the home were owned by various generations of the Vincent family and were generously donated to the Trust. Some of the furnishings are reproductions that were originally on display at Plimoth Plantation. Other items of historical importance are from the collection of the Daughters of the American Revolution. There is also a fruit orchard and an Elizabethan herb garden on the property.

AVAILABILITY:

- Late spring through October: Wednesday through Sunday, a tour of the Vincent House is included in the Architectural Walking Tour of the Vineyard Trust which begins at 10:30am and 2pm. Purchase tickets at The Carnegie (58 North Water St., Edgartown). The walking tour lasts about 90 minutes, beginning at The Carnegie and ending at the Vincent House less than a half mile away. Call to confirm tour times.

NOTES:

- *A bit of information on The Carnegie (58 North Water St., Edgartown)— The Carnegie is where visitors purchase tickets for the walking tour and where the tour starts. The building previously housed the town library, originally funded by Andrew Carnegie. It was recently renovated and opened as the museum of the Vineyard Trust—dedicated to preserving the history of Martha's Vineyard and its people. Visitors should plan to spend some time exploring the excellent exhibits of The Carnegie before or after the walking tour.*

- *Visitors might want to wander down Daggett Street directly across from The Carnegie to watch the Chappy Ferry travel the 527 feet from Edgartown Memorial Wharf to Chappaquiddick Island and back again.*

Photo by Jeffrey Allen. Courtesy of the Nantucket Historical Association.

Greater Light

c. 1790, Artists' Summer Home from 1929

8 Howard Street
Nantucket, MA 02554
508-228-1894
https://nha.org/visit/historic-sites/greater-light/

In 1929, two Quaker sisters from Philadelphia, Gertrude and Hanna Monaghan, purchased this late 18th century barn and transformed it into their artist retreat. Gertrude was a professional artist and Hanna was an actress and author. They were part of Nantucket's thriving art community in the 1920s, 30s and 40s, now referred to as the Nantucket Art Colony.

Greater Light, Gertrude and Hanna's summer home, reflects their eclectic aesthetic. They added unique architectural features and decorative objects. They set about to create a magical space inside and out. Visitors to Greater Light can imagine what life was like for the artists of Nantucket in the early to mid 20th century.

AVAILABILITY:

- Late May through October: daily 11am-4pm. Admission included in the All-Access Ticket available at the Whaling Museum (13 Broad Street).
- Call or check the website for specific dates and details.

NOTES:

- *Greater Light is about a half mile walk from the Whaling Museum.*
- *When visiting the Whaling Museum, do not miss the view of the harbor from Tucker's Roofwalk.*

Hadwen House
1846

96 Main Street
Nantucket, MA 02554
508-228-1894
https://nha.org/visit/museums-and-tours/hadwen-house/

William Hadwen, a wealthy businessman in the whaling and silver industries, built the grand house at 96 Main Street in 1846 for himself and his wife, Eunice. At the same time, William also built the companion house next door at 94 Main Street where various family members would live. Hadwen's Greek Revival mansions were very different from the typical shingled or brick Nantucket houses. These two houses were undoubtedly built to impress with their imposing columns, elevated front porches and grand scale.

William and Eunice entertained the island's elite in style. That tradition was carried on by Joseph Barney when he inherited his uncle's house in 1864. In 1923, Charles Satler and his wife, Maria, bought the house and used it as their summer home for the next forty years. Their daughter donated the house and furnishings to the Nantucket Historical Association in 1963.

The Association restored the house in the 1990s, bringing it back to the days of the mid-1800s. The house provides a glimpse into the privileged lives of wealthy islanders in the heyday of the whaling industry. A guided tour includes the first floor formal parlor complete with a dining table set with china ready for guests and upstairs bedrooms furnished with period pieces. Back downstairs, the Association displays rotating exhibits in the impressive triple parlor. Visitors can appreciate the architectural details of the room—large recessed windows, high ceilings, intricate moldings and massive pocket doors—and imagine how the high society of Nantucket may have mingled in this room while attending one of the many social gatherings held here.

AVAILABILITY:

- Late May through December: daily from 10am-5pm.
- Admission included in the All-Access Ticket available at the Whaling Museum (13 Broad Street). Closed some holidays.
- Call or check the website for specific dates and details.

NOTES:

- *The Hadwen House is less than a half mile walk from the Whaling Museum and directly across from the Thomas Macy House.*
- *When visiting the Whaling Museum, don't miss the view of the harbor from Tucker's Roofwalk.*

Maria Mitchell House
1790

1 Vestal Street
Nantucket, MA 02554
508-228-2896
https://www.mariamitchell.org/visit/mitchell-house

Nestled on a small side street less than a half mile from Nantucket's historic downtown, visitors will find the birthplace of Maria Mitchell, America's first woman astronomer. This modest Quaker house was built in 1790 and acquired by the Mitchell family in 1818. Maria Mitchell was born here on August 1, 1818, living here until she was 18 years old. The house contains many artifacts and personal items of Maria and the Mitchell family, including her telescope.

In 1836, Maria and her family moved to residential quarters on the second floor of the Pacific National Bank in downtown Nantucket. Her father was the Cashier at the bank—a high level position which meant that he was essentially in charge. It was on the rooftop of the bank on October 1, 1847 that Maria discovered a comet with the use of her telescope. For that discovery, she was awarded a gold medal from the King of Denmark. After her discovery, Maria gained national and international fame.

In her lifetime, Maria was a teacher, a librarian and professor of astronomy at the newly-created Vassar College. Maria had a life-long love of learning that is honored and continues through the work of the Maria Mitchell Association—dedicated to providing opportunities for high quality research and learning through the Maria Mitchell Science Center. Today, the Center includes the Aquarium, the Vestal Street Observatory, the Loines Observatory, the Natural Science Museum and the Mitchell House.

AVAILABILITY:

- Mid-June through Labor Day Weekend: Guided tours are available Monday through Saturday, 10am-4pm. Call for schedule for Memorial Day Weekend through mid-June and September through Columbus Day.

NOTE: *Maria is pronounced "Ma-RYE-ah".*

Oldest House/Jethro Coffin House
c. 1686

16 Sunset Hill
Nantucket, MA 02554
508-228-1894
https://nha.org/visit/historic-sites/oldest-house/

The Oldest House is believed to be the oldest residence on Nantucket still on its original site and retaining its original footprint. Coffin family lore says that the house was built in 1686 as a wedding present for 16-year-old Mary Gardner and 23-year-old Jethro Coffin. This was their home for the next 20 years. When they moved off the island, they sold the house to Nathaniel Paddack. Members of the Paddack family occupied the house for the next 131 years.

The house eventually fell into disrepair, but members of the Coffin family with a keen interest in their family history purchased the house and set about to repair it. The Nantucket Historical Association purchased the house in 1923 from Tristram Coffin. A historical restoration of the house was done under the supervision of the Society for the Preservation of New England Antiquities (SPNEA, now known as Historic New England).

In October 1987, the house was struck by lightning and suffered severe damage. Thankfully, after two years of repairs, the house was opened once again, transporting visitors back to 17th century Nantucket. Visitors to the Oldest House can tour all the rooms of the house—the parlor, the great hall, the borning room, the lean-to kitchen and the second-floor bedrooms. The house is furnished with a combination of period pieces and historic reproductions. There is also a historically recreated kitchen garden located behind the house. The Oldest House is truly a hidden gem on Nantucket and one of the finest examples of a 17th century dwelling in the country.

AVAILABILITY:

- Late May through October: daily, 11am-4pm. Admission included in the All-Access Ticket available at the Whaling Museum (13 Broad Street).
- Call or check the website for specific dates and details.

NOTES:

- *The Oldest House is about a half mile walk from the Whaling Museum. A good part of the walk is slightly uphill. The brick and stone sidewalks can be uneven.*
- *When visiting the Whaling Museum, do not miss the view of the harbor from Tucker's Roofwalk.*

Photo by Jeffrey Allen. Courtesy of the Nantucket Historical Association.

Thomas Macy House
c. 1800

99 Main Street
Nantucket, MA 02554
508-228-1894
https://nha.org/visit/historic-sites/thomas-macy-house/

Built around the turn of the 18th century, the house at 99 Main Street was originally a modest house with a front door to the left and two windows to the right. In 1828, Eunice Macy inherited the house from her father's estate. Eunice's husband, Thomas, was a successful businessman whose ventures included owning a candle factory, a large warehouse and shares in various whaling ships. In 1832, the Macys extensively renovated the house, transforming it into the elegant Federal style home that visitors see today. They added 14 feet to the left of the front door, creating an impressive center entrance with intricate molding, shuttered sidelights and a fan detail above the doorway. With the renovations complete, the Macys moved into their house in 1833.

The house stayed in the Macy family for over 100 years. The last of the Macy family to live in the house was Mary Eliza Macy who lived there for more than 30 years until her death in 1931. The house eventually was bought by Jacqueline Garda Stephens Harris around 1947. In 1965, Ms. Harris had an architectural study done of the house and found that very little had been changed since the major renovation of 1832.

It was Ms. Harris's wish that the house be donated to the Nantucket Historical Association upon her death. The Association took ownership of the house in 1987, renovating and updating the house with living quarters upstairs and entertaining space downstairs. The house now serves as event space and lodging for visiting scholars and lecturers. Thanks to the generosity of Ms. Harris, visitors can imagine what life might have been like for a wealthy family living on this beautiful street in the mid-1800s. Visitors can also tour the backyard garden.

AVAILABILITY:

- Late May through October: Included in the Historic House and Gardens Walking Tour leaving daily from the Whaling Museum (15 Broad Street) at 1:30pm. No tours on July 4. Purchase tickets at the Whaling Museum.
- Call or check the website for specific dates and details.

NOTES:

- *Tickets to the Historic House and Gardens Walking Tour may sell out during peak times. Purchase tickets as early in the day as possible.*
- *The one hour guided tour through the streets of historic downtown Nantucket ends with a brief tour of the Thomas Macy House. The walking tour covers about a half mile. The brick and stone sidewalks can be uneven.*
- *When visiting the Whaling Museum, do not miss the view of the harbor from Tucker's Roofwalk.*

Benjamin Nye Homestead
& Museum

c. 1678

85 Old County Road
East Sandwich, MA 02537
508-888-4213
http://www.nyefamily.org

The Nye Homestead was built in 1678 by Benjamin Nye (1620–1706), one of the earliest settlers of Sandwich. He was a farmer, builder and miller, who built the second gristmill in Sandwich in 1669. This home, the second built by Benjamin, was originally designed as a "saltbox", with a long, sloping roof. The house was surrounded by 250 acres of farmland. A substantial renovation of the house was done in the early 19th century by Deacon Silvanus Nye, transforming it into the full colonial that you see today.

Nye family members occupied the house until 1910. In 1957, the house was threatened with demolition. The Nye Family of America Association was able to save the house from the wrecking ball and obtained ownership of the homestead in 1962. Members of the Association worked tirelessly to raise enough funds to restore the homestead. In 1972, the Benjamin Nye Homestead opened as a museum.

The main rooms of the house have been restored to reflect life during different time periods, from the Colonial Era through the 1800s. A guided tour includes two parlors, a late 18th century kitchen, the Nye Marine Room and an early period bedchamber, as well as rotating exhibits. Most of the items on display have been donated by Nye family members. Visitors interested in colonial building practices and the architecture of older houses enjoy peeking into the "Bugaboo Room" where original brick work from the old saltbox house can be seen beneath the main staircase.

The Nye Homestead today is located in a beautiful rural setting with a stream and views out to the salt marshes. Adjacent to the Homestead and also owned by the Nye Family Association are the 1889 East Sandwich Grange Hall and an 1858 mill building under restoration which sits on the foundation of Benjamin Nye's 1669 gristmill. At one time, the road that the homestead sits on was a major thoroughfare leading down Cape. This was once a very busy neighborhood with shops, a post office, a tannery and a tavern.

Today, visitors to the Nye Homestead find a tranquil spot to view the Cape Cod scenery and learn a bit of history at the same time.

AVAILABILITY:

- Mid-June to mid-October: Tuesday through Saturday, 11am-4pm. Closed Sundays, Mondays and holidays.
- Call or check the website for specific dates.

Hoxie House

c. 1675

18 Water Street
Sandwich, MA 02563
508-888-4361
https://www.sandwichmass.org/419/Museums

For well over three centuries, the Hoxie House has sat over-looking beautiful Shawme Pond. It is believed to be one of the oldest saltbox houses on the Cape. This truly remarkable house has survived to this day on its original building site and within its original footprint. While the actual date that the house was built is not known, Reverend Smith and his family began living here in 1675. The house subsequently belonged to seven generations of the Smith family. The house was acquired by the town of Sandwich in 1959 and has been fully restored.

Upon entering the Hoxie House, visitors are immediately trans-ported back to the 17th century. The house has just three rooms and a loft—two rooms downstairs and one bedroom up a narrow, steep stairway. The original architectural features of the house have been maintained including the large hearth, wide plank floors and front door. While the windows have been reproduced, part of an original window is framed and displayed. The loom on display is believed to be one of the oldest in existence in the country. The house has been furnished with period pieces, not reproductions. A visit to the Hoxie House offers visitors the chance to imagine daily life in the Colonial Era.

AVAILABILITY:
- Open mid-June through Columbus Day Weekend: Monday through Saturday, 11am-4:30pm; Sunday, 1-4:30pm.

NOTE: *Nearby and worth a visit are the Dexter Grist Mill (2 Water Street, Sandwich) and the Sandwich Glass Museum (129 Main Street, Sandwich).*

Wing Fort House
c. 1641

69 Spring Hill Road
East Sandwich, MA 02537
508-833-1540
https://www.wingfamily.org/wingfamilyforthouse.html

The Wing Fort House is a bit off the beaten path, but it is worth the effort to find. It is one of the oldest houses in the country owned and occupied by members of one family. Built around 1641, it was the home of Stephen Wing, one of the early settlers of Sandwich. For the next three centuries, the house stayed in the hands of Wing's descendants. The house has been added onto over the years as the needs of each family occupying the house grew. The house was acquired by the Wing Family of America,

Inc. in 1942 from "Cousin Cora" (Cora Wing), the last descendant to own the house. The restored house reflects different historic time periods using Wing family items. Everything that you see in the house has a connection to the Wing family.

A tour of the Wing Fort House includes the first and second floor. The house is furnished with items that bring to life those who lived in the house—their furniture, household items, tools, toys and personal items. Visitors might want to take particular note of the portrait of Mary Gott on the second floor. Mary follows visitors with her eyes as they walk around the room. She even keeps an eye on visitors on the first floor by gazing down at them through a heating grate. It can be a bit unnerving, but it adds to the feeling that the Wing family is still very much represented in this house.

Extensive archeological exploration has been done and continues on the land surrounding the house. Many of the items from these archeological efforts are on display. Given that members of the Wing family occupied this house for centuries, these items offer unique insight into what daily life was like in earlier times.

AVAILABILITY:

- Mid-June through mid-September: Tuesday through Saturday, 10am to 4pm.
- Check the website for opening and closing dates.

Highland House Museum
1907

6 Highland Light Road
North Truro, MA 02652
508-487-3397
http://trurohistoricalsociety.org/highlandhouse/

Visitors who venture almost all the way down the peninsula of Cape Cod can reward themselves with a stop at the Highland House Museum. The Highland House was built as a resort hotel in 1907, marking the beginning of the tourist industry in Truro. Guests were delivered to the hotel from the nearby railroad station by stage coach. Visitors today can only imagine how pleased they must have been to arrive and be greeted by ocean breezes and gorgeous views of the Atlantic Ocean from one of the eastern most points of Massachusetts. Room and board was $8 per day.

With the creation of the Cape Cod National Seashore in 1960, the Highland House and property were incorporated into the National Seashore and came under the purview of the National Park Service. Several years later, the hotel was slated for demolition. Fortunately, in 1970, the Truro Historical Society reached an agreement with the National Park Service to operate the Highland House as a museum dedicated to preserving the history of Truro and its people.

Today, the first floor of the museum houses the Society's extensive collections. There are permanent exhibits dedicated to the history of Truro going as far back as the Native Americans who preceded the earliest settlers. There is a shipwreck room with all sorts of treasures. Visitors learn about the history of the Highland House, railroad service on the Cape and the US life saving stations. Each year, there are new exhibits.

Upstairs, guest rooms are furnished with period pieces which give visitors a feel for what it was like to stay in the hotel. The rooms are reproduced with antique furnishings, bedding, clothing and personal items. The ocean views alone are worth the trip to the "Outer Cape."

Also upstairs, there is a permanent exhibit examining the life of Edward and Josephine Hopper and their deep connection to Truro. Edward Hopper was one of the great American realist painters of the 20th century. His painting, *Chop Suey*, featuring his wife, Josephine, as the model, recently sold at auction for nearly $92 million. The Hoppers spent several months each year in Truro where they owned property and built a studio. Several Truro homes and buildings were subjects of Edward's work and about a third of his work was done in Truro. Josephine was a gifted artist in her own right. While the museum does not have any original works of Edward Hopper in its collection, several pieces of Josephine's work along with some of her personal items are on display.

AVAILABILITY:
- June to September: Monday through Saturday, 10am-4:30pm.

NOTES:
- *A free smartphone audio tour is available.*
- *Highland Light is just a short walk down the road. It is not affiliated with the Highland House Museum. For a small fee, visitors can climb to the top of the lighthouse. There is a children's height requirement of 48" for safety reasons.*

© 2018 STEVEN L MARKOS. *Reprinted with permission.*

Atwood–Higgins House
c. 1730

Bound Brook Island Road
Wellfleet, MA 02667
508-255-3421
https://www.nps.gov/caco/learn/historyculture/
atwood-higgins-house.htm

"Off the beaten path" may be an exaggeration for some house museums, but not for the Atwood-Higgins House. The house is located within the Cape Cod National Seashore off Bound Brook Island Road. There is some conflicting information regarding the exact address of the property. The actual latitude and longitude are listed below. Keep an eye out for a small sign point-ing the way.

The Atwood-Higgins House was built in the early to mid-1700s as a half Cape style house. Additions done in the late 1700s or early 1800s doubled the size of the house to the full Cape house that visitors see today. In 1805, Thomas Atwood, a mariner, bought the house from Thomas Holbrook and Solomon Higgins. In 1919, Thomas Atwood's great-great-grandson, George Higgins, inherited the house and set about restoring it to its original condition. Mr. Higgins never modernized the house, not even installing indoor plumbing. The Atwood-Higgins House is unfurnished, but visitors will tour perhaps one of the best examples of a modest home on Cape Cod that is well over 200 years old—parts of which could be closer to 300 years old.

Mr. Higgins, an amateur historian, built several historically inspired outbuildings on the property including a guest house, a barn and a general store. He hoped to create a historical compound that would be visited by future generations. Mr. Higgins donated the house and property to the Cape Cod National Seashore. Today, the house is open for tours on occasion with reservations. The outbuildings are not generally open to the public. There is some question as to the historical significance of the outbuildings and whether they will be maintained.

AVAILABILITY:

- Open seasonally. Tours by reservation only. Call the Salt Pond Visitor Center (508-255-3421) for information and reservations.

NOTES:

- *Latitude / Longitude: 41.953866, -70.059117*
- *Look for signs on Bound Brook Island Road to the Atwood-Higgins House.*

ADDITIONAL SOURCES:

- Historic American Buildings Survey, Creator, Thomas Atwood, Thomas Atwood, George K Higgins, Charles S Dotts, and Paul D Dolinsky, Robinson, Cervin, photographer. *Atwood-Higgins House, Bound Brook Island Road, Wellfleet, Barnstable County, MA.* Barnstable County Massachusetts Wellfleet, 1933. Documentation Compiled After. Photograph. http://www.loc.gov/item/ma0080/.
- Markos, Steve. "Cape Cod National Seashore/ATWOOD-HIGGINS HOUSE TOUR." National Park Planner. Accessed January 28, 2019. https://npplan.com/parks-by-state/mas-sachusetts-national-parks/cape-cod-national-seashore-park-at-a-glance/cape-cod-national-seashore-historic-sites/sape-cod-national-seashore/.

Captain Bangs Hallet House
c. 1840s

11 Strawberry Lane
Yarmouth Port, MA 02675
508-362-3021
http://www.hsoy.org/historic-sites-alt

The Captain Bangs Hallet House is a lovely Greek Revival style house built in the 1840s. The house was donated to the Historical Society of Old Yarmouth in 1956. The Society restored the house and furnished it with period pieces—some original to the Hallet family—bringing to life the story of Captain Bangs Hallet and the many sea captains that called Yarmouth home.

During the 1800s this house was home to two sea captains, Captain Allen Hinckley Knowles and Captain Bangs Hallet. By 1863, Captain Knowles, living in this modest house, needed a larger one for his family. At the same time, Captain Bangs Hallet who lived nearby was about to retire. He and his wife, Anna, wanted a smaller home. The captains sold their homes to each other, essentially trading houses. The house remained in the Hallet family until after Captain Hallet's death in 1893.

On the first floor, the docent-led tour includes the formal parlor, the second parlor, the dining room, the captain's study and the Exhibition Room which showcases rotating exhibits. Throughout the house, visitors will see many items that tell the story of the voyages of local sea captains to China. They brought back valuable items such as silk, porcelain, tea and spices. The tea and spices were so valuable that they were kept in special locked boxes.

The town of Yarmouth might have been home to more sea captains than any other town in the United States. Many portraits of local sea captains are on display, including that of George Matthews who lived next door. At the age of only 19, George Matthews brought a ship back from New Orleans after the ship's captain and many other crewmembers died of yellow fever.

Upstairs, visitors tour two bedrooms, the Maritime Room and the Asa Eldridge Gallery. In the master bedroom, several items are on display that were owned by Bangs and Anna Hallet, including their bed, the trunk that Anna Hallet took on her travels and other personal items.

In the children's room, visitors can easily imagine children playing with the toys, games and doll furniture. There is a picture of Claudius the Dog over a child's bed. According to Cape Cod lore, a dog named Claudius saved someone who fell overboard. Parents put the dog's portrait over their children's beds to watch over them and keep them safe.

Also on display in the children's room is a rocking horse that was used by the Hallet grandchildren. Captain Bangs Hallet and his wife, Anna, had eight children. Six of their children died in infancy or early childhood. While the death of a child was not an unusual occurrence in the 1800s, it is hard to imagine the loss of so many children. The year 1846 was a particularly difficult time for these parents, losing two children in a span of just months—a seven-week-old child on April 25 and their three-year-old daughter, Marianne, on September 20.

Moving into the Maritime Room, visitors learn about the rich maritime history of the town of Yarmouth. From the China Trade, there are silk cocoons, tea and spices. There are ship models and maritime paintings. Harkening back to the heyday of the clipper ship era, there is a painting of the *The Red Jacket*. This beautiful clipper ship set the speed record for travel from New York to Liverpool, England on her maiden voyage, arriving in 13 days, one hour and 25 minutes. Her captain was a local ship captain named Asa Eldridge.

Other interesting items on display include the rib of a whale killed at Yarmouth Port in 1828, Native American artifacts and whiskey bottles—one still full—found along the nearby beaches dating back to the time of Prohibition. During Prohibition, Canadian ships carried alcohol to the Cape. If they thought they were about to get caught, they would throw the bottles overboard. Perhaps a piece of beach glass found along a Yarmouth beach today could be from one of those bottles.

In the Asa Eldridge Gallery, visitors will see the dress uniform of Brevet Major-General Joseph E. Hamblin. While General Hamblin did not live in this house, his uniform was donated by his family to the Society and has found a home at the Captain Bangs Hallett House. General Hamblin served from the beginning of the Civil War to the end. He died five years after the end of the Civil War at the age of 42. General Hamblin's grave is in Woodside Cemetery less than a half mile from the Captain Bangs Hallet House.

Interestingly, the memorial book written by Deborah Hamblin entitled *Brevet Major-General Joseph Eldridge Hamblin, 1861-65* provides a glimpse of what life was like for General Hamblin and includes many of General Hamblin's personal letters.[2] His letters offer a first-hand account of military life during the Civil War, describing in great detail shelter, clothing, food, marches and battles. He also mentions his homesickness for Cape Cod. In one letter dated October 16, 1862, after receiving a package from home, he writes, "Numberless officers in the Grand Army tender thanks for pleasant indulgences in cake and jellies from Cape Cod. A meager

---

2   Hamblin, Deborah. *Brevet Major-General Joseph Eldridge Hamblin, 1861-65*. Boston: Privately Printed, 1902. *Google Book Search*. Web. 30 September 2015.

110

relic of your bounty is now locked up in a chest constructed for the purpose, now resting at foot of my bed, where I stealthily and miserlike occasionally regale myself with substantial memories of home."[3]

After a tour, visitors should be sure to walk around to the back of the house where they will find a summer kitchen with a brick hearth and a beehive oven—a baking oven that gets its name from its distinctive dome shape—along with a collection of period cooking utensils and household items. Wander a bit farther down the path in the back of the house and step under the canopy of a spectacular 130-year-old weeping beech tree.

---

3   Hamblin, 24.

AVAILABILITY:

- Mid-June to mid-October: Thursday through Sunday, 1 to 4pm. Last tour at 3pm.
- Check the website for opening and closing dates.

NOTES:

- *The Captain Bangs Hallet House sits along what is known as Captain's Mile—an area along Route 6A where 51 sea captains lived. Their homes are marked with a schooner plaque. A brochure with information on each home is available at the Captain Bangs Hallet House.*
- *Gray's Beach/Bass Hole Boardwalk is about 2 miles from the Captain Bangs Hallet House. Head east on Route 6A and take a left onto Center Street. Parking is free. This is a small tidal beach with a boardwalk over the marsh affording wonderful views of Barnstable Bay. It is one of Cape Cod's hidden gems.*

Photo opposite page: Gray's Beach/Bass Hole Boardwalk

Edward Gorey House
c. 1825

8 Strawberry Lane
Yarmouth Port, MA 02675
508-362-3909
http://www.edwardgoreyhouse.org

S et in an early 19th century ship captain's house is a museum
dedicated to the life and work of Edward Gorey—illustrator,
author, set designer, costume designer, puppeteer, animal lover
and all around fascinating character. Anyone who recognizes "A
is for Amy who fell down the stairs. B is for Basil assaulted by
bears..." will love wandering through Edward Gorey's eclectic

house. Visitors who are not familiar with the artist might recognize his most iconic work, the animated introduction to the PBS series *Mystery!* Fan or not, visitors cannot help but leave this house with an appreciation of the creativity of this enigmatic man.

To say that the Edward Gorey House is unique is an understatement. From the outside, the house looks like a typical antique home found on Cape Cod. One indication that this house is anything but ordinary might be the large cat illustration greeting visitors. For most of his life, Edward Gorey summered on Cape Cod. In 1979, after peeking in the windows of this house, he decided to buy it. He lived here full time from 1983 until his death in 2000.

Gorey's work is difficult to categorize. Is it macabre, fanciful, gothic or surrealistic? Gorey himself said, "Ideally, if anything was any good, it would be indescribable." Each year, the museum creates an exhibition based on one aspect of Gorey's work. In addition to that exhibit, visitors can tour the first floor of the house. On display are items from Gorey's life and work—from his childhood to his books to his Broadway show, *Edward Gorey's Dracula*, for which he won a Tony Award for costume design.

Gorey was a voracious collector. At the time of his death, his house contained 25,000 books. Many were bought nearby at the iconic Parnassus Book Service. The weight of Gorey's books actually bowed the floors of the house. The books are now mostly gone, but the house is brimming with items that he collected over the years, from cheese graters to rocks. He kept his collection of round things in his "ball room."

Gorey's kitchen has been left largely as it was when he lived here—cluttered but whimsical. There is a framed waffle on the wall—the last waffle of the millennium from Jack's Outback, a nearby restaurant where Gorey was a regular. At Jack's, regulars sat at their own table, wrote their own orders, chose a mug from the shelf and poured their own coffee. A month of Gorey's orders from June 1998 are framed and titled *A Month in the Life of Edward Gorey at Jack's Outback. (On a personal note—my mother, Elly Belmonte or "Mrs. B" as she was known, was also a regular.)* Edward Gorey became a fixture in the local community. He never married, but he had many close friends.

Always a conundrum, Gorey was often seen wearing a fur coat and yet he was a lifelong animal lover and animal welfare advocate. An avid cat lover, he created the Edward Gorey Charitable Trust to benefit not only cats, but all living creatures including whales, birds, bats, insects and even invertebrates. Through proceeds from the museum, the Trust contributes to many animal welfare organizations.

Visitors can complete a scavenger hunt based on Gorey's *The Gashlycrumb Tinies*. Keep an eye out for little feet poking out from under a rug or a doll falling head first down the stairs. Be sure to spend some time in the wonderful gift shop filled with all things Gorey.

AVAILABILITY:

- Mid-April through June: Thursday, Friday and Saturday, 11am-4pm; Sunday, 12-4pm. July to mid-October: Wednesday through Saturday, 11am-4pm; Sunday, 12-4pm. Mid-October through December: Friday and Saturday, 11am-4pm; Sunday, 12-4pm.
- Check the website for specific dates and special events.

NOTES:

- *Jack's Outback Restaurant has closed, but Jack's Outback II (161 Main Street, Yarmouth Port, 508-362-6690) has opened in its place. The table for regulars is gone, but this new incarnation of Jack's is a very nice local restaurant. It is less than a half mile west on Route 6A from the Edward Gorey House. It is not easy to find. Turn into the long driveway just past the sign for the North Side Nursery School.*
- *Parnassus Book Service (220 Route 6A, Yarmouth Port, 508-362-6420) has been open since 1956. This one of a kind bookstore can be found just a bit west on Route 6A.*
- *Gray's Beach/Bass Hole Boardwalk is about 2 miles from the Edward Gorey House. Head east on Route 6A and take a left onto Center Street. Parking is free. This is a small tidal beach with a boardwalk over the marsh affording wonderful views of Barnstable Bay. It is one of Cape Cod's hidden gems.*

Taylor–Bray Farm
c. 1780

108 Bray Farm Road North
Yarmouth Port, MA 02675
774-251-1869
http://www.taylorbrayfarm.org

Just a half mile off Route 6A, visitors will find Taylor-Bray Farm—a delightful spot with an 18th century farm house, farm animals, an amazing marsh view and history that dates back 10,000 years.

In 1639, Richard Taylor established this farm with his wife, Ruth. The farm was home to seven generations of Taylors for over 250 years. Most notably, Samuel Taylor was born here in 1755. He left the farm as a young man to fight in the American

Revolution. He fought in nearly every significant battle in our country's struggle for independence. He fought in the Battle of Bunker Hill, crossed the Delaware River with General George Washington's men, spent the harsh winter of 1777-1778 at Valley Forge and fought in the Battle of Yorktown which ended with the surrender of the British. After the war, Samuel returned to Cape Cod and his farmland along the marsh. He married his wife, Lucretia, and built the farmhouse which stands today. He began his maritime career and became a successful ship captain.

The farm stayed in the Taylor family until 1896, when it was bought by brothers, George and Willie Bray. After the death of George in 1941, the farm changed hands again. In 1987, the town of Yarmouth bought the farm, preventing it from being sold to developers and preserving this historic property for the enjoyment and education of residents and visitors.

In 2001, the Taylor-Bray Farm Preservation Association was formed by a group of concerned neighbors who recognized the need to protect the farm's unique legacy. The Association works in partnership with the town of Yarmouth and the Historic Commission to preserve and maintain the buildings and grounds and to provide for the care and feeding of the animals.

In 2011, the farmhouse was historically restored and renovated to reflect its 18th century origins. The farmhouse that Samuel Taylor built was originally a two-room deep half Cape style home with a parlor in the front and a kitchen in the back. Some of the boards used in Samuel's house date back to the mid 17th century and are believed to have been reused from the original homestead of Richard and Ruth. The house is furnished with period pieces.

Through a series of grants and countless volunteer hours, extensive archeological work has been done at Taylor-Bray Farm in two distinct areas—the original site of Richard Taylor's 17th century home and the Native American site believed to have been used seasonally by Native Americans around 3,600 years ago. Some Native American artifacts have been found that date back as far as 10,000 years. Research is ongoing.

It is well worth the visit to Taylor-Bray Farm, one of the few remaining working farms on Cape Cod today. Take a picnic and enjoy the beautiful view. Walk the boardwalk into Black Flats Marsh. Say hello to the sheep, cattle, donkeys, goats and chickens. Spring is a good time to see the new baby lambs.

AVAILABILITY:

- Mid-June to December: Check the website calendar for farmhouse tour schedule and special events, including the Spring Sheep Festival.

NOTES:

- *The grounds are open year-round from dawn to dusk.*
- *Do not feed the animals. They are on a strictly controlled diet.*

Photo courtesy of Historic New England.

Winslow Crocker House
c. 1780

250 Main Street (Route 6A)
Yarmouth Port, MA 02675
617-994-6661
https://www.historicnewengland.org/property/winslow-crocker-house/

Mary Thacher was born in 1868 and grew up on Beacon Hill in Boston. She spent her summers in Yarmouth Port with her extended family. The Thacher family has been in Yarmouth since the town's earliest days. Anthony Thacher (c. 1589-1667) emigrated from England in 1635, settling in Yarmouth. When Mary's parents retired to Cape Cod, she and her sister, Martha, relocated with them. After the deaths of both of her parents and her sister,

Mary purchased her own house in Yarmouth Port—the 17th century home of her ancestor, John Thacher (1639-1713), located on the corner of Thacher Street and Route 6A.

Mary had a keen interest in history and antiques. When it came to purchasing antiques, she was not interested in reproductions; she was in search of the real thing. She went to Boston and New York to acquire early American furniture—mostly from the 17th and 18th centuries. She also scoured the many antique shops on Cape Cod for period pieces. She was known to drive a hard bargain. As her collection grew, she wanted to create the perfect place in which to display it. In 1935, she purchased the Winslow Crocker House to do just that.

The Winslow Crocker House was built in West Barnstable around 1780 by Winslow Crocker, a trader and land speculator. The house was grand in size and architectural detail for the time. After Mary purchased the house, it was taken apart piece by piece, moved six miles down Route 6A and reassembled in its current location next to her house on the corner of Thacher Street. The process took ten months. She renovated the house to her liking in keeping with her vision of an early American house while creating the ideal space in which to display her antique furniture, rugs, ceramics and pewter.

Mary donated both of her houses to the Society for the Preservation of New England Antiquities (SPNEA) which is known today as Historic New England. Visitors to the Winslow Crocker House enjoy seeing Mary Thacher's collection of antiques and family heirlooms just as she hoped they would.

AVAILABILITY:

- June 1 to mid-October: Saturday and Sunday, 11am to 4pm. Tours on the hour. Last tour at 4pm.
- Check the website for specific dates.

NOTES:

- *Parking is usually available across Route 6A along the Yarmouth Port common. Take care crossing Route 6A. It is a busy main street.*
- *Captain Bangs Hallet House and Edward Gorey House are located across Route 6A along the Yarmouth Port common.*
- *Gray's Beach/Bass Hole Boardwalk is about 2 miles from the Winslow Crocker House. Head east on Route 6A and take a left onto Center Street. Parking is free. This is a small tidal beach with a boardwalk over the marsh affording wonderful views of Barnstable Bay. It is one of Cape Cod's hidden gems.*

Appendix A

ALPHABETICAL LIST OF MUSEUMS

A

Atwood House & Museum *(Chatham)*
Atwood-Higgins House *(Wellfleet)*

B

Benjamin Nye Homestead & Museum *(Sandwich-East Sandwich)*
Briggs-McDermott House *(Bourne)*

C

Cahoon Museum of American Art *(Barnstable-Cotuit)*
Caleb Nickerson Homestead *(Chatham)*
Captain Bangs Hallet House *(Yarmouth—Yarmouth Port)*
Centerville Historical Museum *(Barnstable-Centerville)*

Cobb House *(Brewster)*
Cooke House *(Martha's Vineyard-Edgartown)*
Cottage Museum *(Martha's Vineyard-Oak Bluffs)*
Crosby Mansion *(Brewster)*

D

Dr. Daniel Fisher House *(Martha's Vineyard-Edgartown)*
Dottridge Homestead *(Barnstable-Cotuit)*

E

Edward Gorey House *(Yarmouth—Yarmouth Port)*

F

Falmouth Museums on the Green *(Falmouth)*

G

Greater Light *(Nantucket)*

H

Hadwen House *(Nantucket)*
Harris-Black House *(Brewster)*
Highfield Hall *(Falmouth)*

Highland House Museum *(Truro—North Truro)*
Hoxie House *(Sandwich)*

J

Jericho Historical Center *(Dennis-West Dennis)*
Josiah Dennis Manse *(Dennis)*

M

Maria Mitchell House *(Nantucket)*

O

Oldest House/Jethro Coffin House *(Nantucket)*
Osterville Historical Museum *(Barnstable-Osterville)*

P

Penniman House *(Eastham)*
Phinney/Jones House *(Barnstable-Barnstable Village)*

S

Swift-Daley House *(Eastham)*

T

Taylor-Bray Farm *(Yarmouth—Yarmouth Port)*
Thomas Macy House *(Nantucket)*

V

Vincent House Museum *(Martha's Vineyard-Edgartown)*

W

Wing Fort House *(Sandwich-East Sandwich)*
Winslow Crocker House *(Yarmouth—Yarmouth Port)*

Appendix B

LIST OF MUSEUMS BY DATE BUILT

1600s

Wing Fort House, c. 1641 with additions over the years *(Sandwich-East Sandwich)*
Vincent House Museum, c. 1672 *(Martha's Vineyard-Edgartown)*
Hoxie House, c. 1675 *(Sandwich)*
Benjamin Nye Homestead & Museum, c. 1678 with substantial renovation in early 19th century *(Sandwich-East Sandwich)*
Oldest House/Jethro Coffin House, c. 1686 *(Nantucket)*

1700s

Osterville Historical Museum, c. 1728 Cammett House *(Barnstable-Osterville)*
Falmouth Museums on the Green, c. 1730 Conant House *(Falmouth)*

Atwood-Higgins House, c. 1730 *(Wellfleet)*

Cooke House, c. 1732 *(Martha's Vineyard-Edgartown)*

Josiah Dennis Manse, c. 1736 *(Dennis)*

Swift-Daley House, 1741 *(Eastham)*

Atwood House & Museum, c. 1750s *(Chatham)*

Taylor-Bray Farm, c. 1780 *(Yarmouth—Yarmouth Port)*

Winslow Crocker House, c. 1780 *(Yarmouth—Yarmouth Port)*

Cahoon Museum of American Art, c. 1782 *(Barnstable-Cotuit)*

Falmouth Museums on the Green, 1790 Dr. Francis Wicks House *(Falmouth)*

Maria Mitchell House, 1790 *(Nantucket)*

Greater Light, c. 1790, Artists' Summer Home from 1929 *(Nantucket)*

Harris-Black House, c. 1795 *(Brewster)*

Cobb House, 1799 *(Brewster)*

1800s

Thomas Macy House, c. 1800, remodeled and expanded in 1832 *(Nantucket)*

Jericho Historical Center, c. 1801, Sea Captain Theophilus Baker's 1801 Home *(Dennis-West Dennis)*

Dottridge Homestead, 1808 (Barnstable-Cotuit)

Osterville Historical Museum, c. 1824, Captain Parker House *(Barnstable-Osterville)*

Edward Gorey House, c. 1825 *(Yarmouth—Yarmouth Port)*

Caleb Nickerson Homestead, 1829 *(Chatham)*
Briggs-McDermott House, c. 1830 *(Bourne)*
Phinney/Jones House, c. 1834 *(Barnstable-Barnstable Village)*
Captain Bangs Hallet House, c. 1840s *(Yarmouth—
Yarmouth Port)*
Dr. Daniel Fisher House, 1840 *(Martha's Vineyard-Edgartown)*
Hadwen House, 1846 *(Nantucket)*
Centerville Historical Museum, c. 1850 *(Barnstable-Centerville)*
Osterville Historical Museum, c. 1855 Herbert F. Crosby Boat
Shop *(Barnstable-Osterville)*
Penniman House, 1868 *(Eastham)*
Highfield Hall, 1878 *(Falmouth)*
Crosby Mansion, 1888 *(Brewster)*
Cottage Museum, late 1800s *(Martha's Vineyard-Oak Bluffs)*

1900S

Highland House Museum, 1907 *(Truro—North Truro)*

Appendix C

LIST OF MUSEUMS BY AREA OF INTEREST

Ancient Houses

Hoxie House *(Sandwich)*
Oldest House/Jethro Coffin House *(Nantucket)*
Vincent House Museum *(Martha's Vineyard-Edgartown)*

Modest Houses

Atwood-Higgins House *(Wellfleet)*
Cottage Museum *(Martha's Vineyard-Oak Bluffs)*
Dottridge Homestead *(Barnstable-Cotuit)*
Harris-Black House *(Brewster)*
Osterville Historical Museum, Cammett House
(Barnstable-Osterville)

Grand Houses

Crosby Mansion *(Brewster)*
Dr. Daniel Fisher House *(Martha's Vineyard-Edgartown)*
Hadwen House *(Nantucket)*
Highfield Hall *(Falmouth)*
Penniman House *(Eastham)*
Thomas Macy House *(Nantucket)*

Maritime History/China Trade

Atwood House & Museum *(Chatham)*
Captain Bangs Hallet House *(Yarmouth—Yarmouth Port)*
Centerville Historical Museum *(Barnstable-Centerville)*
Cobb House *(Brewster)*
Highland House Museum *(Truro—North Truro)*
Josiah Dennis Manse *(Dennis)*
Osterville Historical Museum *(Barnstable-Osterville)*
Penniman House *(Eastham)*
Phinney/Jones House *(Barnstable-Barnstable Village)*

Sea Captains' Houses

Captain Bangs Hallet House *(Yarmouth—Yarmouth Port)*
Cobb House *(Brewster)*

Jericho Historical Center, Sea Captain Theophilus Baker's 1801 Home *(Dennis-West Dennis)*
Osterville Historical Museum, Captain Parker House *(Barnstable-Osterville)*
Penniman House *(Eastham)*

Whaling Industry

Benjamin Nye Homestead & Museum *(Sandwich-East Sandwich)*
Dr. Daniel Fisher House *(Martha's Vineyard-Edgartown)*
Hadwen House *(Nantucket)*
Thomas Macy House *(Nantucket)*

Visual Arts

Atwood House & Museum *(Chatham)*
Briggs-McDermott House *(Bourne)*
Cahoon Museum of American Art *(Barnstable-Cotuit)*
Edward Gorey House *(Yarmouth—Yarmouth Port)*
Greater Light *(Nantucket)*
Highfield Hall *(Falmouth)*
Highland House Museum *(Truro—North Truro)*
Osterville Historical Museum *(Barnstable-Osterville)*

Ornamental Gardens

Cobb House *(Brewster)*
Dr. Daniel Fisher House *(Martha's Vineyard-Edgartown)*
Falmouth Museums on the Green *(Falmouth)*
Highfield Hall *(Falmouth)*
Osterville Historical Museum *(Barnstable-Osterville)*

Textiles

Atwood House & Museum *(Chatham)*
Benjamin Nye Homestead & Museum *(Sandwich-East Sandwich)*
Briggs-McDermott House *(Bourne)*
Centerville Historical Museum *(Barnstable-Centerville)*
Cobb House *(Brewster)*
Josiah Dennis Manse *(Dennis)*

Native American History

Captain Bangs Hallet House *(Yarmouth—Yarmouth Port)*
Highland House Museum *(Truro—North Truro)*
Taylor-Bray Farm *(Yarmouth—Yarmouth Port)*

Science/Astronomy

Maria Mitchell House *(Nantucket)*

Boat Building

Osterville Historical Museum, Herbert F. Crosby Boat Shop *(Barnstable-Osterville)*

Vintage Vehicles

Briggs-McDermott House, Allen Green Carriage House *(Bourne)*
Dottridge Homestead, William Morse Fire Museum *(Barnstable-Cotuit)*

Military History

Captain Bangs Hallet House *(Yarmouth—Yarmouth Port)*
Centerville Historical Museum *(Barnstable-Centerville)*

Archeology

Caleb Nickerson Homestead *(Chatham)*
Taylor-Bray Farm *(Yarmouth—Yarmouth Port)*
Wing Fort House *(Sandwich-East Sandwich)*

Beach Camps

Atwood House & Museum, Nickerson North Beach Camp
(*Chatham*)
Swift-Daley House, A. Thomas Dill Beach Camp (*Eastham*)

Vintage Classrooms

Centerville Historical Museum (*Barnstable-Centerville*)
Josiah Dennis Manse (*Dennis*)

Medical History

Dottridge Homestead (*Barnstable-Cotuit*)
Falmouth Museums on the Green, 1790 Dr. Francis Wicks House
(*Falmouth*)

Antique Tools

Briggs-McDermott House, Alonzo Booth Blacksmith
Shop (*Bourne*)
Harris-Black House, Hopkins Blacksmith Shop (*Brewster*)
Jericho Historical Center (*Dennis-West Dennis*)
Phinney/Jones House (*Barnstable-Barnstable Village*)
Swift-Daley House, Ranlett Tool Museum (*Eastham*)

Farm Animals

Taylor-Bray Farm *(Yarmouth—Yarmouth Port)*

Early Construction Methods

Benjamin Nye Homestead & Museum *(Sandwich-East Sandwich)*
Dottridge Homestead (Barnstable-Cotuit)
Osterville Historical Museum, Cammett House
(Barnstable-Osterville)
Wing Fort House *(Sandwich-East Sandwich)*

Early American Furniture

Winslow Crocker House *(Yarmouth—Yarmouth Port)*

Index

B

L

Lincoln, Clark, 7
Lincoln, Mary Edward, 7-8
Loines Observatory, 82

M

Macy, Eunice, 87
Macy, Mary Eliza, 88
Macy, Thomas, 87
Maria Mitchell House, 81-82
Maria Mitchell Science Center, 82
maritime history, 8, 20, 39, 46, 108-109
   China Trade, 20, 28, 108-109, 136
   clipper ship era, 20, 28, 109
   Crosby family, 16
   shipwreck room, 100
   U.S. Coast Guard, 39
   U.S. life saving stations, 100
   wooden boats, 15-16
Martha's Vineyard, 61-73
Mary Lincoln House, 7-9
medical tools, 12, 54
Mitchell, Maria, 81-82
Mural Barn, 39

44233136R00097

Made in the USA
Middletown, DE
05 May 2019